The Dominie C
Aes
Fables

The Boy
Who Cried Wolf

Retold by Alan Trussell-Cullen

Illustrated by Mike Lacey

DOMINIE PRESS
Pearson Learning Group

Ali was a shepherd boy. Every day he took his
flock of sheep up into the hills above his village.
All day he sat and watched over his sheep.

Sometimes Ali grew tired of having nothing else to do. One day he decided to play a trick on the people in the village below.

"Help!" he cried. "Wolf! Wolf! There's a wolf attacking the sheep!"

The villagers were horrified. They grabbed some big sticks and ran up into the hills to save the sheep from the wolf.

When they reached Ali, he laughed and
laughed. "It was only a joke!" he said.

The villagers didn't think it was funny at all. "We have better things to do than play your silly games!" they said. And they went back down the hill to the village, grumbling all the way.

A few days later Ali was looking after his sheep and feeling bored. He thought he would play his trick on the villagers again.

"Wolf! Wolf!" he cried.

Once again, the villagers grabbed their sticks and came running up the hillside to save the sheep from the wolf. And once again, Ali laughed and laughed.

"I fooled you again!" he said.

Now the villagers were even angrier. "We told you, we have better things to do than play your silly games!" they said. And they went back down the hill to the village, grumbling all the way.

The next day Ali was looking after his flock of sheep on the hillside. Suddenly, he saw a real wolf!

"Help!" he cried. "Wolf! Wolf!"

The villagers heard his cries for help, but they just shrugged their shoulders.

"That silly boy is playing practical jokes again!" they said.

"Help!" cried Ali. "It's a real wolf this time! It really is!"

But the villagers just shook their heads. "As
if anyone is going to believe *him*!" they said.

Ali tried shouting at the wolf. But the wolf wouldn't go away.

He tried throwing stones at the wolf. But the wolf
still wouldn't go away.

Finally, he tried calling the villagers one more time.

"Please help me!" cried the boy. "It really is a real wolf this time!"

The villagers laughed. "That shepherd boy really loves his little jokes," they said.

At that very moment, the wolf rushed at the sheep, snatched up one of them, and ran away with it.

Ali was so upset. He brought his sheep down from the hillside to tell the villagers what had happened.

"It's your fault!" said Ali. "You should have
come to help me!"

"No," said the villagers, shaking their heads. "You brought this all on yourself! We hope you have learned a very important lesson: No one believes a liar, even when the liar is telling the truth!"